Fakultätsvorträge
der Philologisch-Kulturwissenschaftlichen Fakultät
der Universität Wien

Fakultätsvorträge

der Philologisch-
Kulturwissenschaftlichen Fakultät
der Universität Wien

1

herausgegeben von

Franz Römer
und
Susanne Weigelin-Schwiedrzik

William C. Kirby
Harvard University

Chinese, European, and American Universities

Challenges for the 21st Century

7. November 2007

Vienna University Press
V&R unipress

Informationen über die Philologisch-Kulturwissenschaftliche Fakultät:
http://www.univie.ac.at/dekanat-phil-kult/

Kontaktadressen der Institute der Philologisch-Kulturwissenschaftlichen Fakultät:
http://www.univie.ac.at/dekanat-phil-kult/institute.html

Anfragen und Kontakt:
info.pkwfak@univie.ac.at

Bibliografische Information der Deutschen Nationalbibliothek
Die Deutsche Nationalbibliothek verzeichnet diese Publikation in der
Deutschen Nationalbibliografie; detaillierte bibliografische Daten sind
im Internet über http://dnb.d-nb.de abrufbar.

ISBN 978-3-89971-449-0

**Veröffentlichungen der Vienna University Press
erscheinen bei V&R unipress GmbH**

© 2007, V&R unipress in Göttingen / www.vr-unipress.de
Das Werk und seine Teile sind urheberrechtlich geschützt.
Printed in Germany.
Gesamtherstellung: Hubert & Co., Göttingen
Gedruckt auf alterungsbeständigem Papier

Vorwort

In den 90iger Jahren des vorigen Jahrhunderts war oft von einer Krise der Geisteswissenschaften die Rede, zum Teil mit einer solchen Beharrlichkeit, dass schließlich manche Geisteswissenschaftler selbst daran glaubten. Dabei wurde gerne übersehen, dass der Eindruck einer Krise nicht sosehr aufgrund mangelnder Aufgaben und Zielsetzungen entstanden war als vielmehr aufgrund der Schwierigkeit, Inhalt und Methode, Sinn und Zweck der Geisteswissenschaften unter veränderten gesellschaftlichen Bedingungen einer breiteren Öffentlichkeit verständlich zu machen. Dann brachte das Universitätsgesetz des Jahres 2002 für die österreichischen Universitäten neue, stärker an wirtschaftlichen Aspekten orientierte Arbeitsbedingungen und rückte sie mehr denn je in das Blickfeld kritischer Beobachtung, so dass mediale Präsenz, Reputation und öffentliche Wahrnehmung gerade für die Geisteswissenschaften noch mehr an Bedeutung gewannen.

Die im UG 2002 begründete Autonomie ermöglicht den einzelnen Universitäten individuelle, durchaus unterschiedliche Organisationsformen, so dass die geistes- und kulturwissenschaftlichen Disziplinen nicht nur in verschiedener Dichte, sondern auch in den verschiedensten Strukturen repräsentiert sind. Die Philologisch-Kulturwissenschaftliche Fakultät der Universität Wien ist für ein sehr breites Spektrum von Sprachen, Literaturen und Kulturen im europäischen und außereuropäischen Raum zuständig, sie umfasst aber auch Musik-, Theater-, Film- und Medienwissenschaft. Die Strategie der größten Fakultät der Alma Mater Rudolphina zielt – auch im

Zeitalter der Spezialisierung – auf eine möglichst große Breite der an ihr vertretenen Fächer, so dass mehr als ein Dutzend Studienrichtungen, darunter die gesamten Asienwissenschaften (Japanologie, Sinologie, Koreanologie, Indologie, Tibetologie u.a.), in Österreich nur hier angeboten werden. Selbstverständlich darf neben der Breite die Spitze nicht vernachlässigt werden, doch zeigt die Erfahrung, dass gerade die Vielfalt an Disziplinen und Kooperationsmöglichkeiten die Fakultät und die Universität Wien insgesamt für SpitzenforscherInnen von internationalem Niveau attraktiv macht.

Um ihren Aufgaben im Rahmen der neuen Bedingungen gerecht zu werden, hat die Philologisch-Kulturwissenschaftliche Fakultät unter anderem eine Plattform für wissenschaftliche Veranstaltungen ins Leben gerufen, die geeignet sind, einer interessierten Öffentlichkeit ihre Fächervielfalt und Transdisziplinarität sowie die Aktualität ihrer Forschungsschwerpunkte vor Augen zu führen. Mit der allgemeinen Bezeichnung als »Fakultätsvorträge« wird keine Einschränkung auf Vorlesungen und Vorträge im engeren Sinn beabsichtigt, vielmehr ist auch an andere Präsentationsformen wie Podiumsdiskussionen, Konzerte oder Lesungen gedacht. Das Projekt wird von der Hoffnung getragen, dass die neue Veranstaltungsreihe sich bald zu einer eng mit dem Namen der Fakultät verbundenen Institution – oder noch besser: zu einem Identitätssymbol der Philologisch-Kulturwissenschaftlichen Fakultät – entwickeln wird.

Der erste aus der geplanten Reihe der »Fakultätsvorträge« wurde am 7. November 2007 von William C. Kirby (Harvard University) in Anwesenheit des Rektors der Universität Wien gehalten. Sein universitätspolitisch hochaktuelles Thema und seine für die Geisteswissenschaften richtungsweisenden Aussagen fanden reges Interesse und breites mediales Echo, so dass die Fakultätsleitung es für sinnvoll und wünschenswert hielt, den Text auch im Druck zu veröffentlichen. Herrn Professor Kirby sei hiermit für seine bereitwillige Zustimmung und zuvorkommende Mitarbeit sehr herzlich gedankt.

Für die engagierte Betreuung des Projekts ist die Fakultät Frau Dr. Sonja Martina Schreiner ebenso zu Dank verpflichtet wie für ihre sorgfältige Durchsicht der Druckvorlage, durch die das erste Heft der »Fakultätsvorträge« zeitgerecht erscheinen konnte.

Wien, im November 2007
Franz Römer, Dekan

Der Historiker und Sinologe William C. Kirby

oder: Warum wir die Welt ohne China nicht mehr verstehen können

William C. Kirby gehört ohne Zweifel zu den profiliertesten China-Historikern seiner Generation. Seine Lehr- und Publikationstätigkeit ist seit vielen Jahren auf das Engste mit der Harvard University verbunden, entfaltet ihren Einfluss jedoch weit darüber hinaus, vor allem auf den chinesischsprachigen Raum und auf Europa. Diesen Einfluss hat William Kirby ausüben können, weil er seit seiner Studienzeit international orientiert gearbeitet und wissenschaftliche Erkenntnisse hervorgebracht hat, die einen wichtigen Beitrag zur Neuformulierung grundlegender Paradigmata für unser Verständnis der chinesischen Geschichte des 20. Jahrhunderts geleistet haben. Zugleich ist William C. Kirby ein international erfahrener und einflussreicher Hochschuladministrator. Als Dean der Faculty of Arts and Sciences an der Harvard University hat er sich für die Reform der Lehre eingesetzt, um dem einmaligen Ruf dieser Universität mit der Realität einer einmaligen Studienerfahrung zu entsprechen; er hat seine internationalen Erfahrungen eingebracht und sich für die Internationalisierung des Studiums an der Harvard University eingesetzt; er hat die naturwissenschaftliche Forschung und Lehre an seiner Fakultät neu orientiert und zugleich für die Geisteswissenschaften gekämpft. Durch all diese vielfältigen Aktivitäten läuft ein roter Faden: Es ist dies die Auseinandersetzung mit China und seiner Internationalisierung im Laufe des 20. Jahrhunderts.

William C. Kirby hat an höchst renommierten Bildungsinstitutionen in den USA mit früh sichtbarem herausragendem Erfolg studiert, seinen Bakkalaureus am Dartmouth College im Jahr 1972 erworben und zwei Mal in Deutschland studiert, bevor er sich dem Studium Ostasiens zuwandte. Seine Doktorarbeit schrieb er über deutsch-chinesische Beziehungen, und wie es sich für ein herausragendes Frühwerk eines hervorragenden Wissenschaftlers gehört, steckt in Kirbys Dissertation sehr viel von dem, worüber er auch heute noch arbeitet. Sie ist gewissermaßen der Grundstein, von dem aus er Schritt für Schritt die chinesische Geschichte des 20. Jahrhunderts zu seinem Thema machte und Meilensteine setzte, an denen sich das ganze Fach heute orientiert.

Das zentrale Thema dieser Arbeit ist die Frage nach dem internationalen Einfluss auf die inneren Verhältnisse in China nach dem Zusammenbruch des Kaiserreiches und dem von den Großmächten der damaligen Zeit erzwungenen Eintritt Chinas in die Welt der Nationen. Im Sinne seines Lehrers John King Fairbank hat William Kirby immer die Ansicht vertreten, dass der internationale Einfluss von entscheidender Bedeutung für die Entwicklung Chinas im 20. Jahrhundert gewesen ist. Doch gibt es für ihn genauso wenig eine von außen vorprogrammierte Antwort auf die Herausforderung aus dem Westen noch eine ausschließlich aus den inneren Verhältnissen abgeleitete Umbaustrategie der chinesischen Eliten. Vielmehr erfährt der internationale Kontext stets eine den inneren Bedingungen entsprechende Adaption, die bis zum heutigen Tag China so besonders erscheinen lässt. Bei Kirby ist China nicht in erster Linie das viel beschworene Opfer ausländischer Aggression, es ist auch und immer wieder Gestalter des Prozesses der Adaption und Integration von Nicht-Chinesischem in partikular Chinesisches und Subjekt seiner Geschichte mit all ihren Verwerfungen, Irrtümern und Desastern, auch mit den Erfolgen und Wundern, die China immer wieder und nicht erst in der 2. Hälfte des 20. Jahrhunderts zum Gegenstand unserer Bewunderung hat werden lassen.

William Kirby ist nicht nur ein Gelehrter, der in der Lage ist, gegen den Strom zu schwimmen und dennoch ans Ziel zu gelangen. Er ist auch ein passionierter Hochschulreformer, einer, der sich in seiner Funktion als Dekan der Faculty of Arts and Sciences für die Anfänger unter den Studierenden einsetzte, der seine Kollegen fordert, wenn es darum geht, sich in der Lehre zu engagieren, und der selbst sehr engagiert lehrt. Trotz seiner unbestritten herausragenden Position in der China-Forschung war er sich nicht zu gut, Dekan der größten Fakultät seiner Universität zu werden, und auch schon, bevor wir alle ihn kannten, hat er sich Lorbeeren in der Wissenschaftsadministration erworben, so in seiner Zeit von 1980 bis 1991 als Mitglied und späterer Professor der Fakultät für Geschichte an der Washington University in St. Louis.

William Kirby stellte sich Herausforderungen, denen er sich nicht stellen müsste; er verbindet, wo andere trennen; er baut Brücken, wo andere Grenzen ziehen. Kirby arbeitet über China wie Taiwan, über die republikanische Periode zwischen 1911 und 1949 wie über die Volksrepublik China seit 1949. Wiewohl er durch einen Studienaufenthalt in Taiwan mit den dortigen Verhältnissen zunächst besser vertraut war, hat er sich immer wieder forschend mit der VR China auseinandergesetzt und sich mit Problemen beschäftigt, die China gemein sind, egal, ob es von Nationalisten oder Kommunisten regiert wird. Neben Fragestellungen, die eher dem Bereich der politischen Geschichte zuzuordnen sind, arbeitet er sehr erfolgreich und schulbildend an Themen aus dem Bereich der politischen Ökonomie. Er tut dies, so meine ich, nicht, um uns zu beweisen, dass er alles kann. Die Breite seiner Forschung ist vielmehr sein Programm. Er braucht sie, um das zu erreichen, was er erreichen möchte, nämlich eine neu begründete Sicht auf China im 20. Jahrhundert, die mit den eingespurten Paradigmata aufräumt. Allen Vorurteilen zum Trotz sind die Kontinuitäten zwischen der Herrschaft der Nationalisten vor 1949 und der Herrschaft der Kommunisten seit 1949 so groß, dass man über die Grenze des Jahres 1949 hinweg denken muss, um die Entwicklung Chinas im 20. Jahrhundert richtig verstehen zu können. Auch muss man über den Antagonismus zwischen nationalistischer Guomindang und Kommunistischer Partei hinweg denken, um verstehen zu können, wie weitreichend die gemeinsamen Wurzeln dieser feindlich gegenüber stehenden Parteien reichen. Beide Parteien haben sich China im 20. Jahrhundert nicht anders als ein China vorstellen können, in dem Partei und Staat eine untrennbare Symbiose eingehen. Und selbst wenn sie zu den weitest reichenden Reformen fähig sind, halten sie doch letztlich an diesem Modell fest, und zwar mit solcher Überzeugungskraft, dass selbst die aus der Opposition zu diesem System entstandene Demokratische Fortschrittspartei, die heute unter Chen Shuibian Taiwan regiert, sich vom Modell des »Party State« nicht lösen kann. Kirbys Lehrer John King Fairbank hat die Meinung vertreten, dass China in der Kaiserzeit ein Modell der Verbindung von Zentrale und Peripherie hervorgebracht hat, welches seiner Geschichte einen partikularen Stempel aufdrückt und es zugleich zum Vorbild und zur Herausforderung für alle um China herum lebenden Völker machte. Ist der Partei-Staat, ein Staat, der – wie Kirby betont – die politische Ordnung beherrscht, nicht die Gesellschaft, ist dieser Partei-Staat das chinesische Modell des 20. Jahrhunderts, das allen Unkenrufen zum Trotz nicht untergeht, sondern sich nur immer wieder in neuen Farben drapiert?

Die China-Forschung, so wie William Kirby sie betreibt, erforscht China als das andere, weil wir es kennen müssen und im Sinne einer intellektuellen Herausforderungen verstehen wollen. Die Bildungspolitik ist hier ein dankbares Feld. Nur wer sich mit den Traditionen einer Lernkultur auseinandersetzt, auf die China sich heute in seiner Aufholjagd genauso stützen kann wie andere traditionell vom Konfuzianismus geprägte Gesellschaften in Asien, kann verstehen, warum wir unsere Universitäten umbauen müssen. Im 19. Jahrhundert war der Westen eine Herausforderung für China, heute ist es andersherum: China ist die Herausforderung für den Westen. Und die Tatsache, dass China über ein schier unerschöpfliches Heer an jungen Menschen verfügt, die mittels Bildung ihren Erfolg suchen, ist eine Herausforderung, deren weitreichende Auswirkungen leider noch nicht viele verstanden haben. Wenn Bill Kirby in seiner Funktion als Dekan an der Harvard University die Internationalisierung seiner Universität und des Studiums an dieser von vielen bewunderten Stätte des Lernens fordert, wenn er sich bei manch einem Kollegen unbeliebt macht, weil er Zuwendung zu den Studierenden, mehr Zeit für die *undergraduates* und nicht nur Konzentration auf die forschungsorientierten Studenten fordert, dann tut er dies, weil er weiß, dass wir uns einem globalisierten Bildungsmarkt anzupassen haben, der junge Menschen hervorbringt, welche sich der »chinesischen Herausforderung« erfolgreich stellen. Wenn wir lernen zu verstehen, wie China im 20.Jahrhundert den Prozess der Adaption an die internationale Entwicklung vollzogen hat, lernen wir zugleich, uns selbst als Subjekt in den Prozess der Adaption an die Globalisierung einzubringen, mit dem wir gerade zu kämpfen haben.

Als Beispiel hierfür hat Kirby sich das Thema der Entwicklung von Bildung und Wissenschaft in China ausgesucht. Er zeigt uns, dass China sein Bildungssystem in Auseinandersetzung mit den unterschiedlichen Modellen, welche die Welt uns bietet, aus dem Nichts aufgebaut hat, das durch die Abschaffung des kaiserlichen Prüfungssystems im Jahr 1905 entstanden war. Er zeigt, dass die Regierung der VR China sich mit den Eliten einig weiß, dass der Auf- und Ausbau des Bildungssystems für Chinas Wiederaufstieg zur Weltmacht von zentraler Bedeutung ist. Und er macht uns darauf aufmerksam, dass bei aller Konkurrenz auf dem internationalen Bildungsmarkt die Universitäten weltweit vor gemeinsamen Problemen stehen. Die Lösung dieser Probleme kann ohne Einbezug der chinesischen Erfahrungen nicht gefunden werden, und China kann die Probleme seines Bildungssystems nicht ohne internationale Kooperation lösen. Umso wichtiger ist es, dass die Auseinandersetzung mit allem, was heute in China passiert, nicht auf die Spezialisten beschränkt bleibt, sondern als integraler Bestandteil der geistigen Auseinandersetzung mit unserer Zeit die Gemüter herausfordert.

Susanne Weigelin-Schwiedrzik, Vizedekanin

William C. Kirby (Harvard University)

Einleitung zum Vortrag am 7. November 2007

Sehr geehrte Herren, Vizerektor Prof. Dr. Engl und Dekan Prof. Dr. Römer, sehr geehrte Frau Kulturattaché Perez, liebe verehrte Kollegin und Freundin, Frau Prof. Dr. Weigelin-Schwiedrzik, sehr geehrte Damen und Herren!

Es ist mir eine große Ehre und ein Vergnügen, diesen Abend mit Ihnen in dieser alten und ehrwürdigen Universität mitten im Zentrum (oder: im Herzen) Europas verbringen zu dürfen. Wie Prof. Dr. Weigelin-Schwiedrzik weiß, habe ich meine ersten akademischen Schritte im Graduiertenstudium nicht allzu weit von hier, an der Freien Universität Berlin, unternommen. Ich begann dort mein Studium im Jahre 1972 nach meinem ersten Universitätsabschluss in den Vereinigten Staaten dank eines Stipendiums, des damals sogenannten »Luftbrückendank-Stipendiums«.

Berlin, wie das Motto der Stadt damals hieß, war »eine Reise wert«. Doch möchte ich Ihnen versichern, dass für mich die erste Reise von Berlin aus, die eine »Reise wert« war, eine Reise nach Wien war. Ich erinnere mich lebhaft an meine damaligen Selbstzweifel, ob ich nicht doch lieber in die ruhigen Gefilde der einstigen Habsburger Donaumonarchie ziehen sollte als mein Studium in der unsanft geteilten ehemaligen Hohenzollern Domäne fortzusetzen… Ich war damals hauptsächlich nach Berlin gekommen, um deutsche und europäische Geschichte am Friedrich-Meinecke-Institut zu studieren. Das gelang mir auch, doch nicht ohne gewisse Schwierigkeiten, da in jenen Tagen aufgrund intensiver politischer Aktivitäten sich viele Kurse immer noch »im Streik« befanden. Aus diesem Grunde begann ich, mehr und mehr Seminare (und Vorlesungen) zum Thema China zu besuchen, was in jenen Tagen, ungeachtet jeder persönlichen politischen Färbung, als »politisch korrekt« galt. So begann ich, eine neue Richtung einzuschlagen.

Wäre ich damals nach Wien umgezogen, so hätte ich wahrscheinlich mein Studium in Europäischer Geschichte fortgesetzt. Doch auch das ist sicher: wäre ich heutzutage ein Student an dieser Universität, Prof. Dr. Weigelin-Schwiedrziks Präsenz würde mein akademisches Interesse zweifelsohne erneut in Richtung Osten wandern lassen!

Wie auch immer man zu den damaligen Zeitgeschehnissen stehen mag, es war eine Periode intensiver Auseinandersetzung (mit Geschichte und Politik). An der Freien Universität erlaubte mir der bereits fest etablierte Schwerpunkt in Internationaler Geschichte, Asien zu studieren und eine solide Grundlage zu erhalten, auf der ich mein Doktorandenstudium in Europäischer und Chinesischer Geschichte in Harvard fortsetzen konnte.

Chinese, European, and American Universities
Challenges for the 21st Century

Vice-Rector Engl, Dean Römer, Madam Cultural Attaché Perez, and my distinguished colleague and friend, Prof. Dr. Weigelin-Schwiedrzik, Ladies and Gentlemen.

It is a great honor and privilege to be asked to be with you this evening in this great and ancient university, in the center of Europe. As Prof. Dr. Weigelin-Schwiedrzik knows well, I received my first graduate education not far from here, as a student at the Free University of Berlin. I came there as a student in 1972, after graduation from undergraduate college in the United States, thanks to a fellowship then called a »Luftbrückendank-Stipendium.« Berlin, the city's slogan then said, was *»eine Reise wert.«* But you should know that the first travel from Berlin being *»eine Reise wert«* for me was, of course, to Vienna.

I remember wondering if it might have been better to have come to study in the calmer, former realm of the Habsburgs than in the raucously divided former realm of the Hohenzollerns. I had come primarily to study German and European history at the Friedrich-Meinecke-Institut in Berlin, which I did, albeit with some difficulties – for in those days of still-intense political activity many classes were »on strike.« As a result, I started taking more and more classes about China, which in those days, no matter what your political affiliation, could be seen as »politically correct.« Thus I started in a new direction.

Had I come to Vienna then, I might well have stayed in European history. However, were I a student here today, under Prof. Dr. Weigelin-Schwiedrzik, there can be no doubt that I once again would have been swept Eastward.

More than thirty years have passed since then. Thirty years is a short period in the life of your university, founded in 1365, or as we say in my field, in the last years of the Yuan Dynasty. Thirty years is actually a short time even in the life of my own, much younger university, founded just one dynasty later, in the late Ming era. Yet here in Europe the past three decades have seen an unprecedented expansion of higher education and, in the most recent time, efforts at fundamental reform and restructuring. At Harvard, we too have been reforming, indeed overthrowing, our curriculum of the past thirty years, and are in a period of renewal. So we have much to share and much to talk about.

But perhaps nowhere on earth have recent decades seen more revolutionary change in higher education than in the People's Republic of China. As a historian of China, as a scholar trained in Europe, North America, and Asia, and as a recent academic leader in the United States, I have a keen interest in China's higher education reforms and what they mean for all of us.

Let me describe recent trends in China, and then focus on the common challenges to the international world of higher education as we teach those who will lead significant parts of this planet in the 21st century.

Let me start with an example, that of Wuhan University, arguably China's oldest modern university. When we think of Chinese universities in the U.S., we often think only of Peking University, Tsinghua, and a few others. But Wuhan and the surrounding province of Hubei have long been leading centers of commerce, scholarship, and political leadership. It was the great reforming Governor-General, Zhang Zhidong, who founded in 1893 – five years before Peking University – the »Self-Strengthening Institute« that would become Wuhan University. It was in Wuhan that the revolution that overthrew the Qing dynasty in 1912 began. Wuhan would host one of the two contending Nationalist governments in 1927, and the retreating government of Chiang Kai-shek in 1938. It would be an industrial center of the early PRC, and today, western Hubei, upriver from Wuhan, is home to the largest engineering project in world history, the Three Gorges Dam (and even a »Three Gorges Dam University«!)

Wuhan University itself, with a strong history of growth before 1949, and then having been nearly destroyed during the Cultural Revolution, now is a great, comprehensive university, with a faculty of nearly 5,000, teaching a student body of 33,000 undergraduates and 12,000 graduate students; it offers doctoral degrees in 143 subjects.

Wuhan University's renewal and expansion is part of a much larger story of contemporary higher education in China. For China is experiencing a revolution in mass higher education that dwarfs that of the U.S. in the 1950's and of Europe in the 1970's. This is a revolution that began in the final years of the 20th century and is still gathering steam.

Let me try to put it into historical perspective. This is not the first educational revolution in modern China. A little more than a century ago, China underwent a similar, perhaps even more dramatic, seismic shift in educational institutions, when, with the end of the old examination system, the existing structure of local schools, academies, and directorates of study – all linked to the civil service exams – was displaced by a new and dynamic system of public and private institutions.

Then, in the first half of the 20th century, China developed one of the more dynamic systems of higher education in the world, with strong, state-run institutions (Peking University, Jiaotong University, National Central University, and at the apogee of research, the Academia Sinica), accompanied by a creative set of private colleges and universities (Yenching University, St. John's University, and Peking Union Medical College, to name but a few). One institution that developed an international reputation in medical and engineering education, in partnership with Germany, was Tongji University in Shanghai. Sadly, all this would be swept away in the late 1950's and 1960's, yet the traditions and memories of excellence remained, and they have helped to fuel more recent efforts.

Simply in terms of numbers of students educated, the more recent changes are more dramatic even than the great postwar expansion in the United States or the growth of mass-enrollment universities in Europe in the 1970's and 1980's. In 1978, after a decade of mostly closed universities, Chinese universities enrolled approximately 860,000 students. This increased very gradually until 1996, with enrollment then of about one million. In the late 1990's the government decided to greatly accelerate the pace of expansion, and by the year 2000 there were as many as six million students enrolled in Chinese universities.

In the seven years since then, the overall official numbers – counting all kinds of institutions – have risen dramatically. According to the very ambitious 10th Five-

Year Plan of the Ministry of Education, higher education enrollment was scheduled to reach 16 million by 2005 and 23 million by 2010. But, in fact, it has risen even more rapidly, so that the Vice-Minister of Education could tell me last autumn in Beijing that China already had 26 million students in institutions of higher learning.

By contrast the United States had about 13 million undergraduate and 2 million graduate and profession students in 2000, with undergraduates projected to rise to perhaps 15 million by 2010.

China is moving toward mass education. The gross enrollment ratio of the 18-21 year old group is set to be at 15 percent, having been in the low single-digits for most of the history of the PRC. More than that, China plans to enroll as much as 40 percent of young adults in colleges or universities by the year 2020.

I have seen this first hand. A once-small teacher's college, Lin Yi Teacher's University, had 3,500 students in the year 2,000. They now have 35,000. This growth is clear not only in public universities but in the rapidly growing number of private universities. In Xi'an, Xi'an International University (*Xi'an waishi xueyuan*) did not exist 15 years ago; today it has 37,000 students.

To put it in another light, of physical space, the »square meterage« of Chinese universities has more than tripled in the past seven years.

And, in terms of graduates, China now turns out, annually, more PhDs than any other country in the world.

Unlike the American expansion of the 1950's and the European growth of the 1970's, this growth has elements that are also self-consciously elitist, with the aim of building a significant number of world-class universities. These are defined in China as having four characteristics:

being cradles of high-level, creative researchers; frontiers of scientific research; forces capable of transforming research and innovation into higher productivity; and, last, bridges for international and cultural exchange.

To that end the Chinese government and many other sources are providing enormous revenues to the leading institutions. Individual »winners« of recent competitions among universities have been each given several hundred million dollars to expend over the next five years; and runners-up have received funds equivalent to those given »winners« in recent German competitions.

Beyond this, the leading Chinese universities have tapped private and philanthropic and foundation sources for substantial streams of income. Like leading American state universities, such at Berkeley or Michigan, the most prominent Chinese universities know that they will soon be in a position where at most 15 percent of their budget comes from the state; the rest will have to be raised elsewhere.

However these budgets are put together, it seems certain that within ten years the research budgets of China's leading universities will approach those of leading American and European universities – which is to say that they will be *huge* – and that in the realms of engineering and science, Chinese universities will be among the world's leaders.

As an academic leader in the United States, I take this as a welcome challenge to American universities – a challenge both for competition and cooperation.

Although in the latter part of the 20th century American universities were, as a group, among the strongest in the world, there is no reason to imagine that this is a permanent condition.

After all, about a century ago, when China was abandoning the ancient examination system that – just a century earlier – had helped to make China (at least in the West) an ideal of educated, enlightened leadership, almost all of the leading universities in the world were in the German-speaking realm, based on the great 19th century reforms at Berlin, Vienna, and elsewhere. That is why the leading American and Chinese universities – Harvard and Peking University among them – adopted what they thought were German systems by the early 20th century.

And yet – at least according to a recent survey by Shanghai Jiaotong University – today, in the first decade of the 21st century, German universities do not dominate the rankings. Indeed, according to Shanghai Jiaotong University, not one of the top 50 in the world was German (the University of Munich, I believe, was number 51). Now the Germans respectfully disagree! And indeed so do I.

There is, I must say, a real silliness to this rankings game. What is being ranked often has very little to do with education, as distinct from research. Citation indexes vary in usefulness depending on the discipline – in my view extremely important in economics and almost useless in history, just to take two social science disciplines; very useful in chemistry and chemical biology, and without any merit whatsoever in Celtic. Although some in the U.S. try to measure the quality of undergraduate education by teacher/student ratio, and that can indeed be useful, there are few ways of measuring comparatively successful teaching. All of the international rankings focus on research results and prizes, such as the Nobel Prize, and universities glory in having on their faculty

Nobel laureates – and they take credit, in these rankings, for these noble scholars, even though the work that may have gained them a Nobel Prize may have been given for work done decades earlier, and at another university!

Now I must confess that as Dean I never paid much attention to these international rankings – so long as Harvard was ranked number one! For reasons unknown to me, Harvard's reputation is even grander abroad than it is at home. The rankings that I as Dean paid real attention to were on the basis of the surveys we did ourselves, with other colleges and universities in the U.S. And in these, for example, we measured many things, among them »student satisfaction with undergraduate education.« And here I can tell you, we did poorly. That data was very important to me as I endeavored to bring about a broad reform of undergraduate education at Harvard.

But the broader point here in this discussion of rankings is that nothing is permanent in the world of learning. All of us have progressed by learning from one another.

Take again the case of Harvard. My university was founded in 1636, that is, again, in the late Ming dynasty. It is a measure of Harvard's parochialism that no one in Cambridge, Massachusetts, knew that. Nor did we know that the Qing dynasty had been proclaimed that same year (though it would take another eight years to seize power.) Another way to think of it is this: Harvard was founded in a cultural and economic backwater of a Europe that was itself »underdeveloped« in comparison to either the Ming or early Qing.

Harvard became a decent college by copying the norms of British institutions, but even those could hardly compare with the sophisticated Confucian learning of the great Donglin Academy and other institutions of the late Ming and early Qing; and it became a university worthy of the name only in the late 19th century by plagiarizing the policies and priorities of the great European research universities.

Today American and European universities share with our Chinese colleagues many of the same challenges, as all of us look to the world in which we want to extend the promise of higher education while, at the same time, maintaining standards of excellence that are the greatest guarantee that universities will – whether they are state-run or private – serve an important public purpose.

Particularly in an era of mass higher education, we share at least the following challenges:

How do we extend the promise of higher education while maintaining quality?

How do we keep institutions from replicating themselves, and how do we ensure that they will be open to talent and ideas from all sources?

How do we value *teaching* as well as research in an era in which almost all of the rewards, professionally, are in research? (I used to tell my Harvard colleagues: »Without the students, none of you would be here!« They probably didn't believe me, but it's true, and it is true that places with good students, empowered to learn, empowered to challenge the best faculty, are the institutions with the highest quality – and consistently outperform stand-alone think tanks and academies of advance study.)

How do we promote opportunity to recruit and fund the very best students, from all financial, geographic and ethnic backgrounds; and how do we ensure greater levels of access and fairness in the admissions process?

How do we ensure that colleges and universities have the capacity to engage in what you would call here in China self-criticism: to question their organization and their curriculum. Harvard has a good tradition of doing this about once every generation; and although I, for one, would not recommend doing it more often, it is important that in every generation we review what and how we teach; that every generation of faculty have the opportunity to craft a curriculum that it believes in; and that we, as a faculty, define what we believe our students need to know in our time.

How do we ensure that – even though our universities will still be based in a home country, with national responsibilities – we also fulfill our international responsibilities, training students who will be citizens of the world? In my view, and I made this a central point of my deanship at Harvard, American universities have a special responsibility in this historical moment of apparent American influence in the world – a moment, dare I say it, perceived by much of the rest of the world as a combination of American arrogance and ignorance (and perhaps incompetence) in world affairs. At the very minimum, we need to train our students to see our country as others see it.

Finally, beyond the curriculum, we need always to ask the question: why do we have higher education at all? To serve the state? To serve society? To prepare a more educated citizenry? Here our debate goes back minimally to those of the 19th century between proponents of the Humboldtian ideal of *Bildung* (the education of the whole person) as distinct from *Übung* (more practical training), differences that we might phrase today in Chinese as being those between a very broad conception of *jiaoyu* and a narrower, repetitive, *xunlian*.

There is, of course, no one right answer for every time and place, but there may be one American tradition that can contribute to our global discussion of this issue, and that is what has become, over the course of the 19th and 20th centuries, a distinctive aspect of an American undergraduate education. This is a concept of European origin, which has now found its deepest roots in North America. I talk here about the continuing American commitment to the idea of *liberal education*: educating the whole person, not just training the specialist; ensuring that our graduates are curious, reflective, and skeptical learners – people with the capacity for lifelong learning (as their first job will surely not be their last); people who can develop multiple perspectives on themselves and the world, and of whom we can say, when they graduate, they are truly independent of mind.

I can say this with some authority because we at Harvard have just renewed our commitment to this cornerstone of undergraduate education. And we have asked the same question that leaders of Chinese universities in the recent years of reform have asked their institutions: what does it really mean to be an educated person in this day and age?

(Perhaps it is not surprising that at several junctures over the last several years, I have been asked by Chinese colleagues, »What is a Harvard Education, and how can we bring it to China?« Apart from finding it presumptuous to think that I can instruct those coming from a culture with a much longer history of, and dedication to, education than my own, I do not believe in the utility of simple transplants. So when friends from China have asked if they might adopt Harvard's Core Curriculum, I felt obliged to tell them about all its problems and that we were about to replace it.)

I also try to make the point that there has been no single »Harvard education«, but over time a series of models that have been tried, well used, and if necessary discarded, though never without a lot of talk and debate. Last May, when we passed our new curriculum in Harvard College, after seemingly endless discussion, I was reminded of that 1924 debate in the Chinese Communist Party about joining the Guomindang in the first United Front. As the minutes of that meeting were written: »The resolution passed unanimously, even though many comrades were opposed.«

Now, if activities at Harvard and at leading Chinese universities are any guide, one commitment we share is something that is counterintuitive in an age increasingly dominated by science and technology and by pressures for ever earlier and ever greater degrees of specialization. That is our commitment, or re-commitment, to a *general* as well as a specialized education, and a commitment to the *humanities* as part of the core of an undergraduate education.

It is interesting that at a time when European universities appear to be adopting some of the formal structures of perceived international models, such as the U.S. baccalaureate, there appears to be little interest as yet in the educational values that have defined the B.A. in the many American colleges that stress a broad undergraduate education in the liberal arts and sciences.

I am a great admirer of many of the ideals of what has become known as the Bologna Process. It has the promise in time of making higher education in Europe a continental-wide enterprise, with mobility not only of students but also of faculty and staff. That will be critical in competing, and cooperating, with continental-sized systems of higher education in the United States and in China.

My one and perhaps misinformed critique of the process, as I understand it, there is some emulation of the current American concept of baccalaureate, but, unlike the original European baccalaureate, without a common conception of liberal education. More than this, if one looks at the documents of the Bologna, Prague, Berlin, Bergen and other meetings, there is enormous attention paid to research, to funding, to math, science and technology, and precious little to teaching, to citizenship, and to valuing the broad and deep education of the next generation of Europe's citizens. If one looks at the »key competences« for lifelong learning recommended by the European Parliament in 2006, one has, quite appropriately, language learning; information and communication technologies; and math, science and technology. But where are the humanities? Where is the multidisciplinary study of other cultures and religions? Where is education in moral reasoning and philosophy? Where, even, are the »harder« social sciences? I am sure that there are many further discussions to be had of these issues, because the quality of education at the end of the day, is not one simply to be measured in technical or vocational courses; nor can it be measured in incomes earned in Euros, Dollars, or Renminbi. It is measured in people, and their ultimate contribution to society.

What I find so encouraging about Chinese higher education today is the independent understanding that the general education of their students – in the arts and humanities as well as the sciences and social sciences – will be as important to their, and all of our, futures, as will be their specialized, professional training.

Thus today all Peking University students, even in the Guanghua School of Management, have to take a myriad of courses that may include literature, philosophy, and history. And there is an elite liberal arts curriculum in the new Yuanpei Program, named for Peking University's famous German-educated chancellor of the early 20th century, the philosopher Cai Yuanpei, who by the way was a great admirer of Wilhelm von Humboldt.

Chinese educational leaders, at least in the elite institutions, believe that they need to do this, in part because, in China, as in the United States, all the pressures are in the opposite direction – on the part of students, who too single-mindedly pursue their careers, and, on the part of faculty, whose careers and interests are every more specialized – leading to a situation in which students and faculty interact on ever-more-narrow ground.

It would be nice, one of my predecessors as Dean at Harvard once said, if it were true that precisely what the faculty wanted to teach was exactly what the students needed to learn. But that has never been the case, and it is the job of universities to ensure that our students learn broadly, from the best faculty, how to think, to reflect, to analyze, and to become the critical thinkers and problem-solvers of the next generation.

For this, in my view, a study of the humanities is essential. And I find this view shared increasingly today in China. Perhaps this is because educational leaders in China know, better than anyone else, what life can be like in the absence of the humanities, and in the absence of a liberal education. For that is part of the history of China's 20th century.

What happened in China in the past century is perhaps all the more remarkable because China is the world's longest continuous civilization, with the longest continuing sets of philosophical and literary traditions. And it is all the more surprising, because the study of that tradition defined not only what it meant to be a scholar, but what it meant to be powerful. The Qing educational and examination system brought the most learned men in the realm into the service of the state – not because they had been trained in statecraft or tax collection (just the opposite!), but because they had deeply studied what we would today call the »humanities«: because they had studied, memorized, chanted, and metaphorically consumed the classics, and they would, in office, act according to the principles of human behavior that the study of the *Analects, Mencius*, and other great works set out.

There has seldom been a higher academic ideal: good people embarking on the living study of great books in order to do good work in society.

This was the ideal, of course never fully realized in practice, and the ordeal of studying to be a scholar-official was a tortuous one. And there were limits to this system: the absence of the study of mathematics, of science, of practical affairs, did not mean that the Empire was thereby better governed. And their absence arguably contributed to the Empire's feeble capacity, in the 19th century, to respond to a militarized, industrialized, and otherwise energized West, in a series of humiliations that would spell the end of a 2,000-year imperial tradition.

The Qing fell in 1911, but for our purposes the more important date is 1905, when the ancient examination system was ended overnight, and not replaced. From that date – and particularly under Republican and Communist regimes – China would be governed not by a civil service chosen for its proven capacities in moral reasoning, but largely by exemplars of that most dominant and successful Western export, the modern, professional military, in the direct service of another Western export that would not be particularly sympathetic to humanist discourse, the Leninist state.

From that date, and for very understandable reasons, Chinese education at all levels would begin to drift strongly toward the study of those subjects that would bring about a return to *fu qiang*, »wealth and power,« primarily mathematics, science, and engineering.

And within a decade of that date, the moral foundation of both Chinese government and culture, Confucianism, would come under a withering attack, leaving a void in the realm of human and social values that has only started to be re-filled in recent years.

In the absence of the humanities, there were arguably two dominant themes in education. One, by no means limited to China, was the belief that in an age of science one could quite literally engineer a bright future, a new people. This was the dream of Chinese leaders from Sun Yatsen onward, of a government of technocratic expertise, capable of »reconstructing« China with roads, railroads, and dams – a government of huge ambition, as seen in the early dreams and later realization of the Three Gorges Dam project. In short, this is the belief in the power of technology to develop a country.

This reflects, and probably reinforces, the nature of China's leadership: Among the seven members of the 15th Standing Committee of 1997-2002, under the leadership of President Jiang Zemin, all but one was certified in engineering. Jiang's own love of, and support of the automobile industry may be traced to his traineeship at the Stalin Automobile Works in Moscow in 1955. Jiang's energetic premier, Zhu Rongji, graduated in electrical engineering from Tsinghua University. Of the nine members of President Hu Jintao's Standing Committee (2002-2007), all nine, including Hu, had engineering education backgrounds and working experience as engineers. (The recently announced, new Standing Committee does have two members with some training in the law – whether the ascendence of lawyers to power is a good thing remains to be seen!)

Sun Yatsen had once translated the term, »technocracy« as »the dictatorship of the engineers.« Now, I like engineers. Some of my best friends are engineers. But here is perhaps no more fitting description of the contemporary government of the PRC. Where else do we see such a marriage of political power and engineering ambition?

To the management of internal waterways, an ancient Chinese speciality, has been brought the most advanced, even audacious, technology. The Three Gorges Dam project – which will make the once isolated wartime capital of Chongqing a great, international, ocean-going port city – was conceived by Sun Yatsen in the 1920's. It has now been built. Of all the world's governments in the early 21st century, only China's has the engineering imagination, political will, and financial resources to complete a project of this scale and to physically relocate inhabitants in its way. (I recall a *China Daily* headline of a few years ago, after one of the massive relocations of villagers on the banks of the Yangzi: it crowed, » 300,000 Happy Peasants to Move!«)

Similar levels of determination may be seen in urban settings. Take the case of Shanghai. Communism was at first a lethal preservative for Shanghai. In 1987 one could shoot a movie (»Empire of the Sun«) in Shanghai set in 1937, and not worry about the background. But after decades of stagnation the city has been re-imagined, re-planned, largely rebuilt and utterly reborn. Where else on earth can one imagine the construction, in fifteen years' time, of five subway lines, two major tunnels and three bridges over a large river, a massive elevated highway system, and an airport the scope of which may not be matched anywhere, not to mention a magnetic-levitation train to get you there. One can agree or disagree with the decisions to pursue any of these projects (which are but the highest profile ones among many thousand more), but not, I think, with the idea that they are the result of an engineering state unleashed and unchecked.

A second belief of the 20th century was that »culture« and the arts were to be firmly subordinated to the purposes of the developmental state. Under Chiang Kai-shek's »New Life Movement« and Mao Zedong's »Cultural Revolution,« the humanities were mobilized for the purposes of the state. As Mao Zedong put it, literature and art were to be defined as »the artistic crystallization of the political aspirations of the Communist party.« There was, Mao said, no such thing as art for art's sake. His wife, Jiang Qing, who in the 1930's had been a minor film actress in Shanghai, working under the not-so-revolutionary name of »Blue Apple,« was by the 1960's the most ardent proponent of cultural dictatorship, of »cultural revolution.« And for ten years, every drama, opera, film, and story that did not conform to her conception of revolutionary art was withdrawn or suppressed – including virtually every significant work of traditional and modern art.

The purpose of art was that people should find in art and literature their models for daily, revolutionary, life.

Well, as the great 20th century writer Lu Xun once observed: »All art may be propaganda; but not all propaganda is art.«

What is my point here? It is simply this. Chinese history in the first three-quarters of the 20th century shows what dislocation can ensue when a civilization loses its cultural foundations, its moral compass, on a relentless quest for wealth and power. In that quest, China imported all sorts of Western »isms«: scientism, militarism, Leninism, chief among them; and it denigrated nearly every aspect of a civilization that, just a century earlier, was the most sophisticated and accomplished on Earth.

Today, a more self-confident China is beginning to re-explore its past and making that past part of its modern education. There are many signs of a new cultural pluralism in today's China, and of a fundamental willingness to imagine and build institutions of learning which are at the forefront of science and technology, yet also find the means to honor and promote the humanities. I personally take it as a positive sign that statues of Confucius are replacing statues of Mao – even though their works may still be equally unread.

Perhaps the most important revolution in Chinese higher education today will not be its size and scope, but the fact that, even under the leadership of engineers, leading institutions have come to understand that an education in the absence of the humanities is, at the end of the day, an incomplete one. This is a recognition that, in an age still, perhaps necessarily, consumed with *fu qiang*, that as countries vie for power, and as individuals seek to accumulate wealth, an education that stresses the values that make for a strong, and even harmonious human community are more important than ever.

Let me make it clear that I speak here not only about China, but also about my own country, whose own pursuit of wealth and power in recent years may have come at some considerable cost to its moral fiber.

Just weeks before he was assassinated, President John F. Kennedy captured the essence of the humanities in a speech at Amherst College. He spoke about poetry, but his idea applies to all the creative disciplines:

> When power leads man toward arrogance, poetry reminds him of his limitations. When power narrows the areas of man's concerns, poetry reminds him of the richness and diversity of his existence. When power corrupts, poetry cleanses, for art establishes the basic human truths which must serve as the touchstone of our judgment.

And in speaking as I have of the challenges facing higher education in China, Europe, and the United States in this era of attempted reform and renewal, I mean to speak of our collective human experience. After all, as Confucius said, »We have myriad diversities, but one *Dao*.«